HOW OUR BODIES WORK

FOOD AND DIGESTION

JAN BURGESS

Editorial planning
Philip Steele

SILVER BURDETT PRESS

Copyright © 1988 by Schoolhouse Press, Inc.
an imprint of Silver Burdett Inc.
Prentice Hall Building, Route 9W,
Englewood Cliffs, N.J. 07632

Original copyright, © Macmillan Education Limited 1988
© BLA Publishing Limited 1988

Designed and produced by BLA Publishing Limited,
East Grinstead, Sussex, England.

A Ling Kee Company

Illustrations by Sebastian Quigley/Linden Artists; Sallie Alane
Reason and Linda Thursby/Linden Artists
Printed in Hong Kong

88/89/90/91/92/93   6 5 4 3 2 1

Library of Congress Cataloging-in-Publication Data

Burgess Janet, 1952–
    Food and digestion.
      (How our bodies work)
    Includes index.
    Summary: Discusses the function of the digestive system, the
importance of food, and the consequences of poor nutrition.
      1. Nutrition — Juvenile literature. 2. Digestion —
Juvenile literature. 3. Gastrointestinal system —
Juvenile literature. [1. Nutrition. 2. Digestive system]
I. Title. II. Series.
QP141.B98   1988
612'.3   88-518

ISBN 0-382-09704-1 (hardback)

Photographic credits

t = top b = bottom l = left r = right

cover: Trevor Hill

4 The Hutchison Library; 5 S. & R. Greenhill; 6*t* Michael
Holford; 6 The Ancient Art and Architecture Collection;
7 Vivien Fifield; 8 Vision International; 9*t* Tesco Stores
Ltd; 9*b* Trevor Hill; 10*t* S. & R. Greenhill; 10*b* ZEFA;
12 Vision International; 13*t* Biophoto Associates;
13*b* Frank Lane Picture Agency; 14*t* Bruce Coleman
Limited; 14*b* Vision International; 16*t* S. & R. Greenhill;
16*b* Vision International; 21*t*, 21*b* Science Photo Library;
22 Sporting Pictures; 25*t* Science Photo Library;
25*t* Vision International; 26 Sporting Pictures; 28 Trevor
Hill; 29 S. & R. Greenhill; 30 Vivien Fifield; 31*t* Biophoto
Associates; 31*b* Vision International; 32*t* The Hutchison
Library; 32*b* Colorific; 33 Oxfam; 34 RHM Centre;
35*t* Vision International; 35*b* S. & R. Greenhill; 36 Vision
International; 37*t* S. & R. Greenhill; 37*b* Camilla Jessel;
38 National Dairy Council; 39*t* Vision International;
39*b* Science Photo Library; 40 Biophoto Associates;
41 ZEFA; 42 Trevor Hill; 43*t* S. & R. Greenhill;
43*b* Vision International; 44 Science Photo Library; 45
Eric & David Hoskings

How To Use This Book:
This book has many useful features. For example, look at the table of contents. See how it describes each section in the book. Find a section you want to read and turn to it.

Notice that the section is a "two-page spread." That is, it covers two facing pages. Now look at the headings in the spread. Headings are useful when you want to locate specific information. Next, look at a photograph, drawing, chart or map and find its caption. Captions give you additional information. A chart or map may also have labels to help you.

Scan the spread for a word in **bold print**. If you cannot find one in this spread, find one in another spread. Bold-print words are defined in the glossary at the end of the book. Find your bold-print word in the glossary.

Now turn to the index at the end of the book. When you have a specific topic or subject to research, look for it in the index. You will quickly know whether the topic is in the book.

We hope you will use the features in this book to help you learn about new and exciting things.

Contents

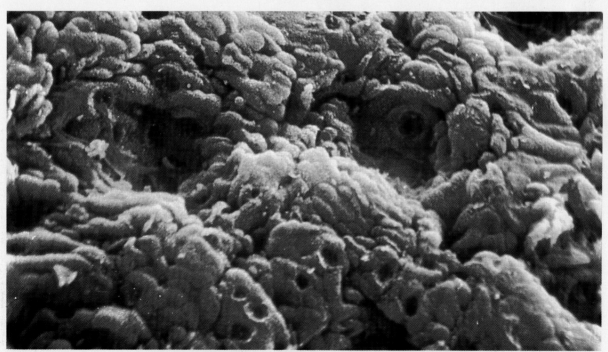

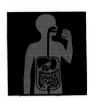

Introduction

If you had to make a list of your ten favorite things, you would probably put in something to eat or drink. We all enjoy the smell of fresh bread, the taste of an ice-cold drink on a hot day, or munching on a crisp apple. Eating is something most of us enjoy. It is also necessary to eat to stay alive.

Of course, humans are not the only things that must eat and drink. The meat and vegetables we use for food were once living animals and plants themselves. Every living thing needs food.

Small animals, such as rabbits or birds, catch and eat insects or smaller animals. In turn, these animals become food for larger creatures. When the larger animals die, their bodies break down and go into the soil.

Plants make use of the substances that are broken down into soil to help them grow. Plants become food for animals, and the process begins again. In this way, the plant and animal worlds are linked together. Each depends on the other for food and growth.

▼ A field of wheat is harvested in the late summer sunshine. All life on the earth depends on the sun. The sun's light and warmth makes plants grow. Animals eat the plants, or they eat other animals which eat plants.

The Food Connection

If we made a list of which animals feed upon what, our list would soon become a complex pattern. Parts of a plant might be eaten by a mouse and an insect. The insect might be eaten by a lizard, and the mouse by a snake. A bird of prey might eat the insect, the mouse, the lizard, and the snake. This pattern is called a **food web.**

Within a food web, there are several **food chains**. A food chain is one path in the web. For example, tiny plants in a tidal pool are eaten by a sea snail. The snail might be eaten by a crab. The crab might be eaten by a squid which, in turn, is eaten by a fish.

Plants are usually at the bottom of a food chain. They are food for a great number of animals. Humans are usually at the top of a food chain. Very few animals get the chance to eat us.

The Food We Eat

Food supplies the body with energy, or the power to do things. In this book, we will learn about substances in the food which provide that energy. They are called **nutrients**. We will find out about the way in which the body takes in food and uses it through **digestion**. It is important to understand about food and digestion, because a healthy life depends upon healthy eating.

▲ This is a food network. Tiny plants and creatures that drift in the sea are eaten by larger creatures and small fish. These fish are eaten in turn by larger fish. The larger fish may be caught by seabirds or by humans.

► A family sits down to a meal in China. They are eating noodles, bean sprouts, seafood, and fruit. Human beings eat both plants and animals. People in different parts of the world like to cook their food in different ways.

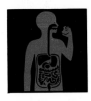

Hunters and Farmers

▼ The first farmers lived in the river valleys of the Middle East and North Africa. This ancient Egyptian painting shows scenes from a harvest. Each year, the Nile River flooded the desert. The floods left behind a layer of mud. Crops could be grown in this rich mud.

Humans are the only animals that can grow their own food. All other creatures must gather it or hunt for it. They may search for seeds, nuts, and berries. They may catch other animals.

It was like this for the first people on the earth. They gathered parts of the plants that they found growing, or they trapped wild animals. Every day, a lot of time was spent just finding enough food to stay alive. Early people moved from place to place. When all the food in one area was used up, they moved on. People still live in this way in some parts of the world.

▼ Thousands of years ago, people had to hunt wild animals for their food. They painted pictures of the animals they hunted.

Crops and Animals

Later, people learned how to save some of the seeds they had picked for food. They planted them each year, and waited for the plants to grow. They could be sure of having food later in the year. This meant that they could settle down and live in one place. They caught and tamed wild animals. Some of these animals could provide a regular supply of milk and meat to eat or hides and wool to make clothes.

A Hard Life

A bad winter or a dry summer meant that crops would not grow properly. Early farmers had to grow enough food to last them through the times when they could not grow anything.

It was difficult to make the food last. People found that meat, fruit, and vegetables could be dried in order to stop them from spoiling. Salt, too, could be used to **preserve** food for the long winter months. Foods could also be pickled in a liquid such as vinegar.

New Machines

For hundreds of years, even people who were not farmers grew some vegetables and kept a few animals for food. Then, people started to live in big cities. There was no space there to grow food. Farmers had to grow more food to feed the people who lived in the cities. Farmers soon learned better ways of growing crops and storing them. Machines were invented to do the farm work more quickly. New roads and railroads were built to take the crops to markets in the cities. Ships were built to carry food from one country to another.

In many countries today, only a few people grow crops or keep animals for their own food. Most people go to a store to buy food that has been produced to sell.

▼ In the 1700s and 1800s many types of machines, like this mechanical corn reaper, were invented. Farmers could now grow more crops and harvest them more quickly. Food was sent to the evergrowing cities to be sold.

Food Today

One hundred years ago, there were only 1.6 billion people in the world. Today, there are nearly 5 billion. Many people die because they do not have enough to eat. Many more go hungry. Enough food is grown in the world to feed everyone. The main problem is that crops do not always grow in the places where they are needed most.

How do farmers try to keep up with the growing demand for food? Twenty years ago, an acre field of wheat gave three quarters of a ton of grain. Today, it gives twice as much. This is partly because farmers use **fertilizers** to make the soil richer. Fertilizers contain the **chemicals** which plants need to grow well.

Farmers, too, use poisons called **pesticides**. These kill off insects which might eat the crops we need for food. Farmers have also been helped by the development of large farm machines. Now, fewer people are needed to grow and harvest more crops. Farm work is much quicker.

◄ Today, machines are often used to harvest fruit and vegetables. This machine is being used to help with the pineapple harvest in Hawaii. As the field workers pick the fruit, they place it on the conveyor belt.

Keeping Food Fresh

Once a crop has been harvested, it does not stay fresh for long. It soon starts to spoil. This is because it is being broken down by tiny creatures called **bacteria**. Some bacteria are harmless, but others can make people sick if they eat them. There are many ways of keeping food fresh, so that it lasts longer.

We still use old methods such as drying, salting, or pickling food. All these methods keep the bacteria from destroying the food. Food also keeps better if it is kept cold. **Refrigeration** slows down the rate at which bacteria can work. Another way of preserving food is by **irradiation**. Rays are passed through food in order to kill the bacteria. Irradiation is a fairly new method. Tests are being done now to make sure that it is completely safe.

▲ Supermarkets offer a wide range of products. Food on the shelves has come from all over the world. It comes in a great variety of packages.

The Food We Buy

A hundred years ago, most people ate fresh meat, fish, and vegetables. They bought the food and prepared it themselves.

Today, many people eat food that has been treated in some way or **processed**. Once the crops have been harvested or the animals killed, they are taken to factories. There, the food is cleaned and sorted. Then, it may be chopped, mashed, frozen, dried, or put in airtight cans. Often, it is cooked and made into food that is ready to eat, such as pies, cookies, or breakfast cereals. After the food has been put into packages or canned, it is sent to stores and supermarkets.

◄ Bacteria cannot break down food quickly in cold conditions. Home refrigerators and freezers make it possible for us to keep food fresh for long periods.

Food and the Body

Cars need gasoline to make them go. A fire needs wood or coal before it can burn. Gasoline, wood, and coal are all types of fuel. The fuel that makes your body work is the food you eat. You use it up as you work, play, sleep, and grow.

Your body is made up of billions of tiny parts called **cells**. Every single cell needs food to stay alive.

The Food Processor

Food enters your body at one end when you eat it. Unused parts of the food pass out at the other end when you go to the bathroom.

In between, there is a long tube called the **digestive tract**. This tube is made up of several **organs**, or body parts that do specific jobs. The food that we eat cannot be used right away by the body. It passes through the digestive tract, where it must be mixed, mashed, and broken up. Then the nutrients in the food can be used by the body.

▼ The body is a wonderful machine. It breaks down the food we eat and takes out the nutrients we need to live.

▲ Playing can use up a lot of energy! Food is the fuel which keeps us going.

Digestion starts as soon as you take a bite of food. Your teeth crunch the food into small pieces. The liquid in your mouth, called **saliva**, mixes with the food. Once the food has been swallowed, it passes down to the bag-shaped organ called the **stomach**. Here, more liquids mix with the food. It is broken up into even smaller pieces.

The next part of the digestive tract is called the **small intestine**. Here, the food is squeezed and churned into its smallest pieces. Nutrients pass out through the walls of the small intestine into the blood which carries them around the body. The nutrients are stored in the **liver**.

Food waste, which the body cannot use, is left behind. It passes into the next section of the digestive tract, the **large intestine**. Here, water is taken from the waste and it becomes solid. The waste is finally pushed out of the body.

When you drink a liquid, your body takes in the water it needs to stay alive. Water is also squeezed into your blood from the food you have eaten. The amount of water in your blood is controlled by two filters called **kidneys**. Waste water is then passed from the body. It is called **urine**.

The Digestive System

Mouth: Teeth chew up food. Saliva makes it slippery and starts to break it down.

Esophagus: The tube through which food passes from the mouth to the stomach.

Liver: A nutrient storage area and chemical factory.

Stomach: Juices mix with the food. They contain further chemicals to break it down.

Kidneys: Clean liquid waste and pass it out of the body.

Small intestine: Nutrients pass through the wall of this tube into the blood.

Large intestine: Last stages of digestion. Water is squeezed from the waste.

Rectum: The end of the large intestine, through which solid waste is passed from the body.

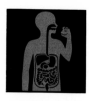

What Is Food Made Of?

▼ Bread fuels the body with carbohydrates. They give us the warmth and energy we need. Carbohydrates in bread, cereals, rice, and potatoes take the form of starch.

All substances are made up of tiny parts called **molecules**. The food we eat is made up of very large molecules. The process of digestion tears these molecules apart. The food is turned into simple nutrients which are made up of smaller molecules. These small molecules can be carried easily in the blood and can be used by the body's cells.

The Energy Givers

Most kinds of food contain many different nutrients. Some nutrients are known as **carbohydrates**. They provide much of the body's fuel. Carbohydrates are usually found in the kinds of food we find

filling, such as bread, rice, pasta, and potatoes. This type of carbohydrate is called **starch**. **Sugar** is another type of carbohydrate. Often, food containing starch has other nutrients in it, too. The foods which supply us with sugar have very few other nutrients.

Inside the body, starch and sugar, which are very complex, are broken down to form a very simple type of sugar called **glucose**. Glucose is a fuel needed by every cell in the body. In the blood, glucose joins with the gas **oxygen** from the air we breathe. Together, glucose and oxygen release the energy needed to power your body.

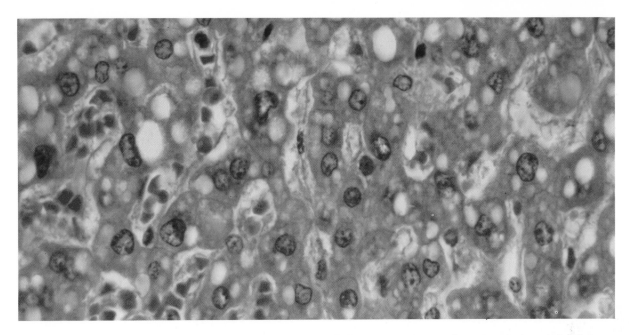

▲ The fats we eat quickly pass into the bloodstream. They give us energy. Here droplets of fat are collecting in the liver.

▼ The crew of a trawler raise their catch. Fish gives us plenty of protein. Protein helps the body grow, and also gives us energy.

Fats are also energy givers. Like carbohydrates, they are broken down inside the body and used as fuel. Small amounts of fat are also needed for body growth. Any extra fat may be stored as a layer of fat on your body. Eating too much fat is bad for your health.

Fats are found in red meat, lard, margarine, and oil, and in dairy food such as milk, butter, cheese, and yogurt. Cakes, candy, and cookies also contain fats.

The Body Builders

Proteins are another type of nutrient. They contain a chemical called **nitrogen**. Nitrogen is needed to build new cells and to repair old ones. Children need to eat plenty of protein because their bodies are still growing. Protein is found in meat, fish, cheese, and eggs.

Our bodies cannot store extra protein for future use. Any protein that is not needed is passed out of our body in urine.

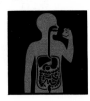

Food at Work

Food contains other substances that we need in order to stay healthy. **Dietary fiber**, or roughage, comes from green, leafy vegetables, the skins of fruit, and husks of grain. It is not digested in the body, and it does not pass through the walls of the intestine. Even so, it plays its part in keeping us healthy. Fiber gives bulk to the food which passes down the digestive tract. This bulk helps the intestines to push the food along. Fiber exercises the intestines and keeps them strong.

▲ Leafy vegetables give us dietary fiber. This helps to move food through our intestines. Vegetables, like spinach, also give us vitamins and minerals, such as calcium and iron.

▼ Being out in the sun can make your body produce vitamin D. Vitamin D is also found in the fats and oils that we eat.

Releasing Energy

There are many kinds of chemicals found in the foods we eat. Some of them are not turned into energy directly. They help the body in other ways. Some of these are known as **minerals**. A mineral called **calcium** is found in milk. It helps to strengthen our teeth and bones. **Iron** is another mineral found in foods. It helps the blood to carry oxygen.

Some of the other chemicals are called **vitamins**. Vitamins help to release the energy from carbohydrates, fats, and proteins. There are several vitamins and each does a different job. Vitamin K, for example, helps parts of the blood clot together, so that it does not continue to flow from a wound.

Vitamins and minerals do not have to be broken down by digestion. They are carried in the blood to the liver. There, vitamins are stored until they are needed.

▼ This chart shows the full range of vitamins and some of the foods in which they are found. It also shows which parts of the human body are helped by which vitamins.

Vitamin	found in ...	good for ...
A	dairy products vegetables fruit	skin, ears, nose, throat, eyes
B₁ thiamine	grains bread dried beans	digestion, carbohydrate control
B₂ riboflavin	poultry dairy products red meat	skin, oxygen for cells
Niacin	red meat fish dried beans bread, cereals	nervous and digestive system
Vitamin C	citrus fruit green vegetables tomatoes	teeth and gums, action of minerals
Vitamin D	milk dairy products fish cod-liver oil	bones and teeth, controls calcium and phosphorus
Vitamin E	vegetable oil grains meat (especially liver)	cell tissues
Vitamin K	vegetables grains	blood clotting

Biting and Chewing

Our bodies get ready to digest food before we even take a bite. The smell and sight of food makes saliva squirt into our mouths. The saliva is a chemical produced by three pairs of **salivary glands**. These glands lie at the back of your mouth and under your tongue. They make over a quart of saliva every day.

Saliva is the first of many liquids that mix with the food on its way through the digestive tract. These juices contain chemicals called **enzymes**. Enzymes work on the food, and break it down into simple parts. The enzyme in saliva acts on starch. Saliva also softens food, so that it can be swallowed more easily.

▲ When you bite into a sandwich, you use your incisors. Your other teeth then grind up the bread, so that it can be swallowed.

◄ Scraps of food leave bacteria on your teeth. The bacteria make an acid which can eat into the tooth's outer covering of enamel. This can make the tooth decay. Tooth decay can be very painful. It can cause cavities. You should brush your teeth carefully after each meal, to keep them clean and healthy.

Breaking up the Pieces

Teeth break up large pieces of food. They make them small enough to be swallowed. Humans can eat a wider variety of foods than almost any other animal. We can do this because our teeth have different shapes.

The sharp, square teeth at the front are called **incisors**. They are used for cutting, chopping, and biting. At the sides of the incisors are pointed teeth called **canines**. They are used for tearing food. The teeth at the back are big and flat. These **molars** have top surfaces which are wide and ridged. They grind the food into a smooth mixture. Once the food is well chewed and mixed with saliva, the tongue rolls it into a ball. The ball of food is pushed to the back of the mouth. It is ready to be swallowed.

All the teeth are rooted firmly in the two powerful **jaws**. The movements of these jaws allows us to use our teeth. Each tooth is protected by a hard, white covering. Beneath this is a bone-like substance. The center of each tooth is made up of a soft pulp.

Humans have two sets of teeth. The first set start to come through when a baby is about six months old. They are called the milk teeth. There are twenty-four milk teeth. At the age of five or six, the milk teeth begin to fall out. A new set of thirty-two adult teeth begin to grow in behind them.

▼ Digestion starts in the mouth. Our teeth prepare the food for swallowing. They must be very strong to keep chewing day after day, year after year. Here, you can see what a tooth looks like inside and the position of the teeth in the jaw.

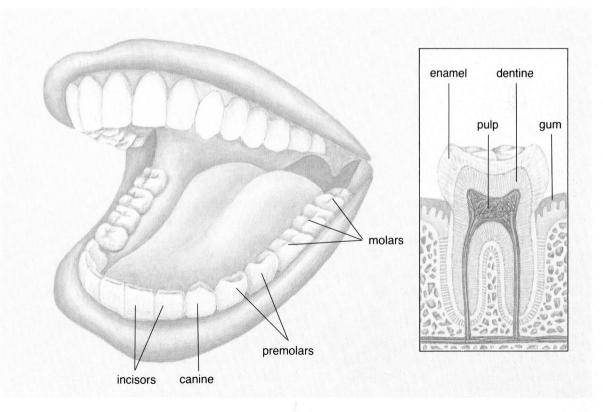

enamel dentine

pulp gum

molars

premolars

incisors canine

Swallowing Food

▼ Your mouth is used for breathing as well as for eating. A system of trapdoors makes sure that the air passages do not become blocked with food when you swallow.

Breathing   Swallowing

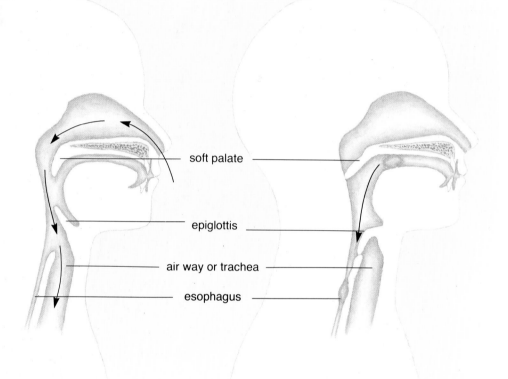

soft palate

epiglottis

air way or trachea

esophagus

A tube called the **esophagus** leads down into the stomach from the back of your throat. At the top, the esophagus opens up into the back of your nose. When you swallow, this opening is blocked off by a flap of skin called the **soft palate**.

Lower down, the esophagus opens into the tube that takes air into your body. When you swallow, this opening is also closed off by a trapdoor called the **epiglottis**. This keeps food from going down into your lungs. If food does enter

the wrong tube, it makes you choke. Choking pushes air out of your body very fast. This blast of air pushes the food back to the top of the esophagus or to the mouth.

Food does not just drop down the esophagus. Waves of movement squeeze it along. The movements are made by **muscles**. The muscles start to tighten and relax as soon as food enters the esophagus. That is why you can swallow even if you are standing on your head.

Into the Stomach

At the end of the esophagus is a strong ring of muscle called a **sphincter**. This keeps food which has passed from the esophagus to the stomach from being squeezed back. Your stomach is located higher up in your body than you might think. The picture below shows just where it is.

The wall of the stomach is muscular and stretchy. At its smallest, the stomach holds about one half quart. After a big meal, it might hold as much as two quarts.

Once food has reached the stomach, the process of breaking it down goes more quickly. Liquids called **gastric juices** pour into the stomach. They are made by glands in the stomach wall. The gastric juices contain more enzymes that work on the food. They also contain a chemical called **hydrochloric acid**. This acid is so strong that it could eat into the stomach itself, as well as the food. The walls of the stomach are protected from the acid by a jelly-like lining called **mucus**.

During and after a meal, the stomach gives a squeeze about every twenty seconds. This churns up the food and allows the gastric juices to mix thoroughly. A small amount of the nutrients in the food pass through the stomach wall into the bloodstream. However, most of the food passes into the small intestine.

▼ Food is squeezed through the esophagus into the stomach. If you could see inside your body, you would find that the outside of your stomach is smooth. It is strengthened by powerful muscles. Inside, the stomach wall is lined with mucus.

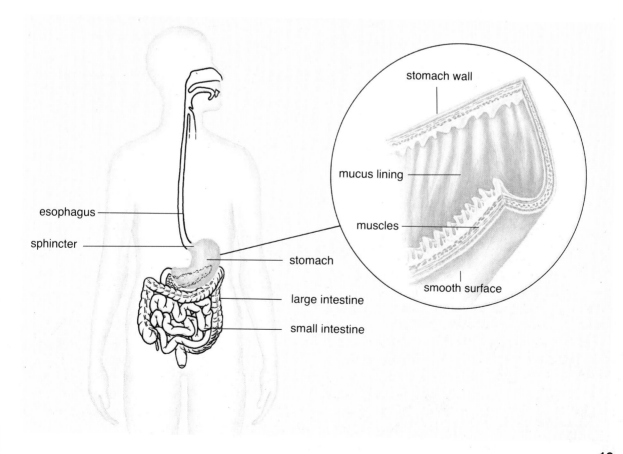

Into the Blood

Most food in the stomach is ready to move on after an hour or two. There is another sphincter between the lower part of the stomach and the small intestine. It is usually closed. However, the sphincter relaxes from time to time. Each time it relaxes, a little half-digested food passes through it, from the stomach and into the small intestine.

The Small Intestine

The whole digestive tract is about thirty feet long. The small intestine alone is about twenty-one feet in length. The first part of the small intestine is called the **duodenum**. Here, more juices attack the food. They contain a rich mixture of enzymes made in an organ called the **pancreas**.

Other chemicals are added to the mixture from the **gall bladder**. The gall bladder pours out a green liquid called **bile**. Bile acts on droplets of fat. It breaks up large droplets of fat into many tiny ones. This makes it possible for the enzymes to reach the fat and break it down.

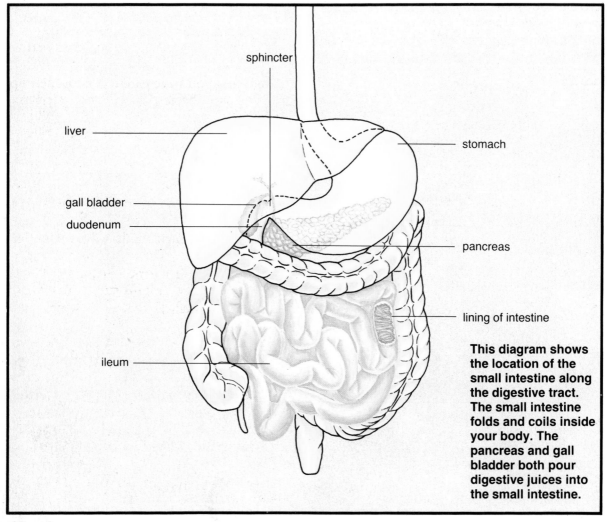

This diagram shows the location of the small intestine along the digestive tract. The small intestine folds and coils inside your body. The pancreas and gall bladder both pour digestive juices into the small intestine.

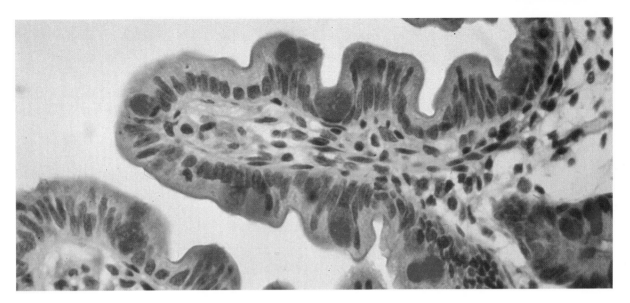

▲ Millions of villi stick out into the small intestine like tiny fingers. Almost all the nutrients that have been digested are taken into the villi. Along with blood vessels, each villus contains tiny tubes which take in some of the fats that have been digested.

▼ This is a microscope picture of green bile breaking fat down into smaller droplets, so that they can be absorbed into the body.

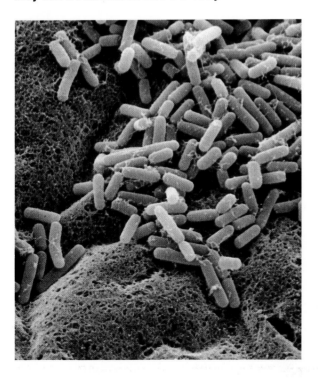

Passing on the Nutrients

The food passes from the duodenum to a part of the small intestine called the **ileum**. Here, digestion is nearly completed. No matter what you have eaten, it is broken up into the same basic parts. These parts are small and simple enough for the body to use them as fuel or as the building blocks for new cells.

Nutrients from the digested food now pass through the wall of the small intestine. The inside of the intestine is covered with millions of tiny, finger-like bumps. These are called **villi**. Each villus waves about in the food mixture. There are so many villi that if they were spread out, they would cover a tennis court! This means that there is a huge surface through which the nutrients can pass into the blood.

Inside the intestine walls there are masses of tiny tubes called **capillaries**. They carry blood in and out of the body tissues. The walls of the capillaries are only one cell thick. Nutrients from the intestine can squeeze through the tiny space between the cells and pass into the blood. Blood is the body's transportation system. It carries the nutrients away from the intestine to wherever they are needed.

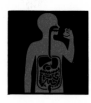

The Liver

Blood vessels are tubes which carry blood. The tiny blood vessels which lead from the small intestine join up to form larger and larger ones. They all join together to make a blood vessel called the **portal vein**. This leads to the liver. The blood flows away from the intestine along this vein. It carries most of the nutrients from the digested food to the liver.

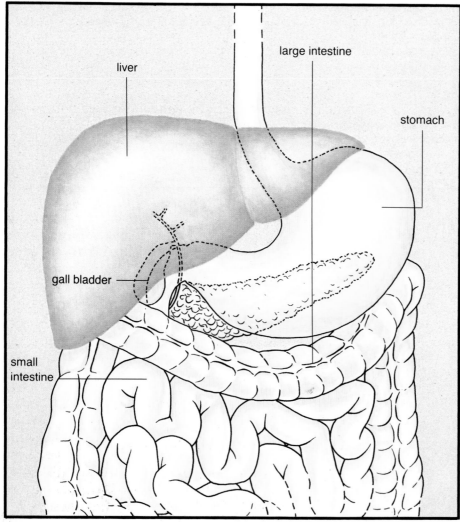

liver

large intestine

stomach

gall bladder

small intestine

▲ Some glycogen is stored in our muscles. When we call on our muscles to do some hard work, like these athletes, the glycogen is turned quickly into glucose. The glucose is used as a fuel to release the energy we need. More reserves of fuel can be called up from the liver. Glycogen can be turned into glucose by the liver, also.

◄ The liver of an adult weighs about three and one-third pounds. It is found next to the stomach. It separates the digested nutrients which enter the blood. Some are sent to be used by the body. Others are sent to be stored around the body. The liver can hold enough glycogen to keep the body going for about six hours.

Central Storage

The liver has many jobs to do. It acts as a storage place for nutrients. It sends them out to the parts of the body that need them.

Most of the carbohydrates you eat are broken down into glucose. Your body needs a steady supply of glucose to keep it going. However, we do not have to keep eating carbohydrates all the time. Glucose can be stored in the liver as a substance called **glycogen**. Between meals, the liver is busy turning glycogen back into glucose for instant use. Glucose is carried in the bloodstream to every cell in the body.

Some of the fats we eat are needed for building new cells. The liver sends out any extra fat into the blood. In the long term, it is stored as body fat. However, it can be changed back into body fuel when the body runs out of carbohydrates.

Protein from the food we eat is broken down into **amino acids**. The body cannot store amino acids. Instead, the liver takes out the amount needed for the moment. Any extra amount passes to the kidneys. It becomes **urea**. Urea is passed from our bodies in our urine.

Bile is made in the liver. It is piped from the liver to the gall bladder. It is stored there until it is needed to digest fats in the duodenum. Vitamins and iron are stored in the liver. Old blood cells go to the liver to be broken up and destroyed.

Central Heating

A great many chemical processes are going on in the liver all the time. These processes give off heat. The liver is like a central heating boiler which keeps the body warm. Heat from this boiler is carried around the body in the blood vessels which act as the pipes of the central heating system. This is how our bodies are able to stay at the same temperature when it is hot and sunny or snowing outside.

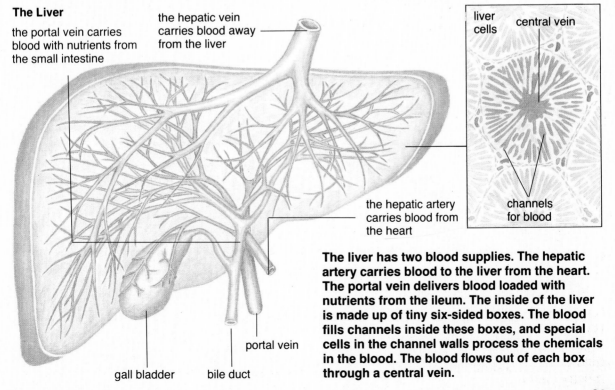

The Liver

the portal vein carries blood with nutrients from the small intestine

the hepatic vein carries blood away from the liver

liver cells

central vein

channels for blood

the hepatic artery carries blood from the heart

portal vein

gall bladder

bile duct

The liver has two blood supplies. The hepatic artery carries blood to the liver from the heart. The portal vein delivers blood loaded with nutrients from the ileum. The inside of the liver is made up of tiny six-sided boxes. The blood fills channels inside these boxes, and special cells in the channel walls process the chemicals in the blood. The blood flows out of each box through a central vein.

The Large Intestine

▼ The large intestine, or colon, is much wider than the long, twisting small intestine. A meal may pass through the small intestine in five or six hours, but it may stay in the large intestine for a day or more.

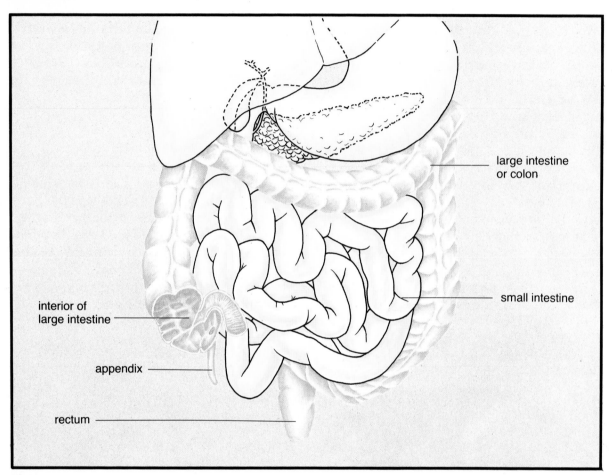

large intestine or colon

small intestine

interior of large intestine

appendix

rectum

Back in the digestive tract, the remains of food are being passed from the ileum to the large intestine, or **colon**. It is called the large intestine because it is wider than the small intestine. It is only four and one half feet long, so it is much shorter than the small intestine.

The remains of the food enter the large intestine a little at a time. By the time food reaches the large intestine, most of the digested nutrients have passed into the blood. All that is left is waste, which is mostly made up of dietary fiber. There is also a lot of water mixed in with it. This water is now taken out of the waste through the walls of the large intestine.

The waste now reaches the end of the large intestine, which is called the **rectum**. By now the waste is very dry and solid. It passes out of your body when you go to the bathroom.

If plenty of fiber is eaten the waste is bulky and travels quickly through the large intestine. If too little fiber is eaten the waste travels more slowly. This can cause health problems, such as constipation.

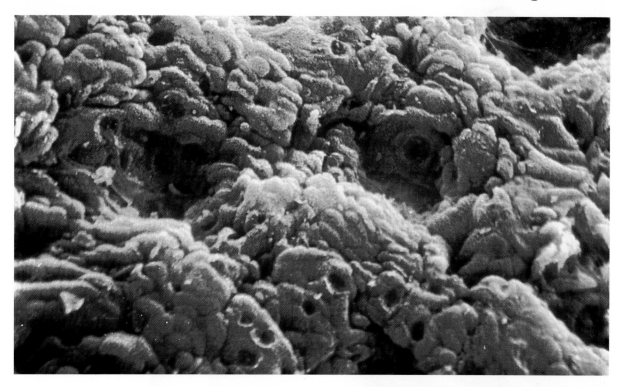

▲ The wall of the large intestine has strong muscles. Waves of movement push the bulky waste along to the rectum. Water squeezed from the waste is passed into the blood through the wall of the large intestine.

Wash Your Hands

The large intestine is home to a large number of bacteria. Most of them are harmless to us. Some are helpful. They help to break down the food and some can help make useful vitamins which are taken into the body through the intestine wall. However, some of the bacteria are very harmful. Therefore, it is important to wash your hands well after going to the bathroom. All traces of germs must be removed.

By the time your breakfast has reached the large intestine, it is probably time for lunch. During lunch, the digestive process begins again. The digestive process goes on smoothly, day and night. You do not have to think about it at all.

▲ Always wash your hands well after going to the bathroom. The germs of some diseases pass out of the body in waste matter. You could catch the disease, and pass it on to someone else if you are not careful.

The Kidneys

Humans can survive for several days without food. However, we cannot do without water for more than two or three days. Water provides half of our total body weight. An adult's body contains about twenty quarts of water. All the cells in the body contain water. There is water in the spaces between the cells, as well as in the blood and other body fluids.

Important substances, such as salts and nutrients, are carried in water. In fact, all the chemical changes that go on inside us happen in water.

Water is taken into our bodies and passed out again as we eat, drink, breathe, sweat, and go to the bathroom. It is very important that the right amount of water is taken in and passed out.

The water balance of our bodies is controlled by a kind of meter in the brain and in the digestive tract. If our bodies lose even one tenth of their water and we do nothing to replace it, we begin to feel very sick.

◄ Our bodies are using up and losing water all the time. If we lose just five percent of our total water, we feel thirsty. If we lose twenty percent, we die. This can happen after only two or three days without water. Water leaves our bodies as sweat or urine.

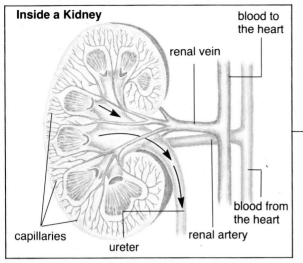

Inside a Kidney

blood to the heart

renal vein

capillaries

ureter

renal artery

blood from the heart

▲ Inside each kidney, there are millions of tiny blood vessels and many tiny tubes. Water and wastes from the blood are filtered as blood passes from the vessels into the tubes.

▶ Urine passes to the bladder through the ureter. When the bladder is only a quarter full, our brain tells us that we need to go to the bathroom.

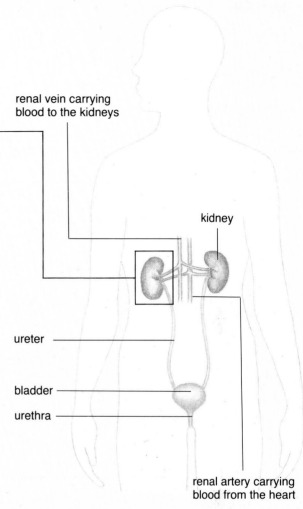

renal vein carrying blood to the kidneys

kidney

ureter

bladder

urethra

renal artery carrying blood from the heart

The Cleaning System

One important way that water is removed from the body is in urine. Urine contains any extra water that the body does not need, together with wastes taken from the water in the blood. Urine is made in the kidneys. We have two kidneys. They are found close to the main blood vessels which run down the center of our bodies. Blood passes through the kidneys. There, it is filtered, as though it were passing through a fine sieve. Some of the water from the blood, together with unwanted chemicals and poisons, pass through the filter.

Precious chemicals and cells which the body needs are left behind. Most of the water with these chemicals and cells is then returned to the blood. A small amount of water containing the waste chemicals and poisons is left. This is the urine.

Waste Water

The urine flows from each kidney through a tube called a **ureter**. The tubes lead to the bag-like **bladder**. As the bladder fills up with urine we feel the need to go to the bathroom. The urine leaves the bladder through a tube called the **urethra**. Each day, we pass out about a quart of urine. It may be slightly more or slightly less. This depends on how much we have had to drink, and whether we have lost water in other ways, such as by sweating.

All the blood passes through the kidneys to be cleaned almost 300 times in a single day. If one kidney stops working, the other one can still do the job on its own.

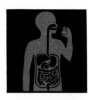

Input and Output

▼ If we eat the wrong food or too much food without exercising, we can become fat. Being overweight can put stress on the heart and on some bones. It can also make us feel uncomfortable.

Fuels provide energy. Energy gives machines the power to do things. Food is the fuel that provides your body with energy. Energy allows the body to work. Energy is measured in units called **calories**. Different kinds of food contain different amounts of calories.

How Much Food Do We Need?

An eleven-year-old girl uses up about 2,200 calories of energy in a normal day. She has to eat food containing roughly the same number of calories if she is to keep her body fit and healthy.

If the girl eats food with more calories than she needs, the extra food is stored as fat. She will put on weight. If she eats food with fewer calories, then any stores of fat already there will be used up to supply her body with energy. She will get thinner.

We know when to eat and when to stop.

Part of the brain tells us when we are hungry or full. Most children balance the amount of food they eat each day with the amount of energy their bodies use up without any problem.

However, people do not always eat only when they are hungry. Sometimes, they eat just because it is time for a meal. The sight, smell, or taste of food tempts people to eat food they do not really want. If people eat more than they need over a long period, they often become fat.

Being much too fat or much too thin is very bad for your health. If people choose to eat only certain types or amounts of food, they are on a **diet**. People who are too fat often go on diets. Sometimes, people diet too much. They eat so little that, eventually, they can no longer eat a normal amount. They become very thin and sick. This disease is called anorexia.

Input	Calories	Output for one hour	Calories
cup of tea, with milk and sugar	40	watching television	85
1 tsp. sugar	18	reading	85
1 boiled egg	90	writing	115
cup of milk	150	bicycling fast	600
2 bacon slices	300	soccer	650
3 slices of bread	240	tennis	450
4 oz. chocolate	575	basket ball	550
2 hot dogs	400	jogging	600
8 oz. steak	390	hiking	400

▲ Here you can see the number of calories provided by various kinds of foods. Also, you can see how many calories are used by the body during one hour of exercise.

▶ The best way to keep our weight down and to stay fit is to exercise. Hikers use their leg muscles. The muscles use up more energy than usual. They take it from the body's food stores.

Burning It Off

When a car travels fast, it uses up gasoline more quickly than normal. The same is true of our bodies. Exercise, such as swimming or bicycling, uses up calories more quickly than pastimes such as reading or watching television. The safest way to get rid of extra fat is to increase the amount of exercise you do, rather than decreasing the amount of food that you eat.

ELKHART LAKE I M C

29

A Poor Diet

The word diet also describes the range of food that a person eats. A person may have a healthy or a poor diet. Sometimes, people have a diet which supplies all the energy they need and yet they still become sick.

This is because our bodies need a whole variety of nutrients to stay healthy. A lack of even tiny amounts of vitamins and minerals can cause serious diseases.

Becoming Sick

Three hundred years ago, the only way to travel from one continent to another was by a long sea voyage. It was very difficult to keep food fresh for months on end. The sailors had to live on hard biscuits and small amounts of salted meat. Often, they became sick, and even died from a disease called scurvy.

Then, it was discovered that eating fresh lemons, oranges, and limes prevented scurvy. Although they did not know it at the time, the sailors were suffering from a shortage of vitamin C. Eating citrus fruit supplied their bodies with this vitamin.

◄ Sailing ships of 300 years ago take on provisions on the North American coast. British sailors became known as limeys because they ate limes to prevent scurvy. Scurvy can be prevented by eating fresh fruit and vegetables which contain vitamin C.

In many countries today, a lot of people suffer from **malnutrition**. This means that the food they eat does not contain the right variety of nutrients for good health. Malnutrition can occur even when there is plenty of food, if that food is all the same. For example, there may be only rice or corn to eat, which do not provide all the necessary nutrients.

Children are especially at risk from malnutrition because they are growing. A lack of vitamin D can cause a disease called rickets. The child's bones become soft, and they do not grow properly. A lack of vitamin B may cause a disease called beriberi. A person with beriberi becomes very thin and has swollen legs and feet.

In the developed countries today, most people have plenty of food to eat. Unfortunately, people in these countries do not always realize that it is important to eat all kinds of different food. Always choosing the same food, or eating too much processed food, can be unhealthy.

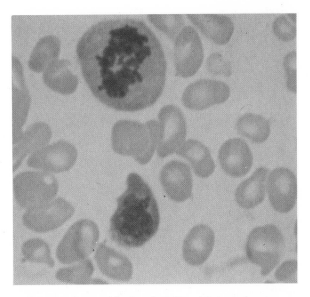

▲ There are two kinds of cells which make up blood. White blood cells help the body to fight disease. Red blood cells carry oxygen from our lungs throughout the body. To do this, they need iron. If we do not take iron into our bodies, we may suffer from a disease called anemia. Some of the blood cells shown here have been starved of oxygen because of anemia.

Extra Vitamins

Fresh food contains the highest amount of vitamins and minerals. Vitamins can be lost if food is stored for a long time before it is eaten. Also, they can be lost if the food is overcooked.

Sometimes, food manufacturers add extra vitamins to foods that do not have them. For example, vitamin D is often added to milk. Some stores sell vitamin and mineral tablets to people who think that they may not be getting enough in their food. However, the best way to make sure you do get enough vitamins and minerals is to have a good, balanced diet.

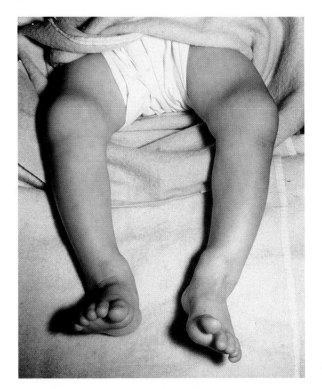

◄ Vitamin D can be found in fish oil, milk, and egg yolk. A shortage of vitamin D can lead to a disease called rickets. Children with rickets have soft bones. Their legs may become misshapen. The best way of preventing the disease is to make sure that children get plenty of the foods which contain vitamin D.

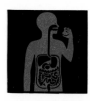

Not Enough Food

▼ In places like North Africa there is very little rain. The land is dry and dusty. Water for the people, animals, and crops has to be collected from deep wells. Sometimes, there is no rain and the wells dry up. The crops do not grow. The animals and people starve.

The human body cannot survive long without food. Every day around the world, about 35,000 people die because they do not have enough food to eat. Many of them are children.

At the same time, in other countries, there is often more food than can be eaten. Whole "mountains" of grain and "lakes" of milk are put into storage. Thousands of tons of fruit and vegetables are thrown away or fed to animals.

Why do so many people in the world go hungry? In some places, there is a shortage of water, so that crops cannot grow. Sometimes, the soil is washed away by sudden floods. Often, people do not have enough money to buy food from outside the area. Sometimes, governments get people to grow crops to make money, rather than for food. Sometimes, wars keep people from growing their crops.

▲ So much wheat has been harvested in this farming town in Nebraska that the grain has been piled up on the main street. While some countries produce too much food, other countries have shortages.

▲ Welsh children join a walk-a-thon to raise money to help people starving in other lands. Organizations such as CARE or U.N.I.C.E.F. can send emergency food supplies. They can set up long-term projects to help the farmers in these countries.

Helping Out

Sometimes, when a large number of people are starving, food is sent to hungry people by those countries which have a surplus, along with money and medical aid. There are many groups in these countries which collect money from people, so that it can be used to help the starving people of the world.

Food supplies help in the short term. They may keep people from starving during a **famine**. In the long run, however, the people must be helped to produce food for themselves. A supply of clean water, tools for farming, and seed may be more important than gifts of food. There are many organizations which work with people to help them prevent food shortages. One of these organizations is called Oxfam.

Helping in North Africa

Dogani Bere is a village in Mali, in North Africa. For several years, there was little or no rainfall. The villagers of Dogani Bere went hungry. In 1984, a worker from Oxfam came to the area to see what could be done to help. Later, Oxfam helped the villagers to build two small dams. Oxfam raised money for the villagers to buy vehicles and cement. It gave the villagers some expert advice.

Today, the dams are finished. They enable the villagers to store water so that there will be enough to water the crops the next time there is no rain.

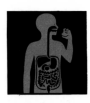

The Wrong Kind of Food

Having too much food causes problems, too. In some parts of the world, there is so much food that many of its useful parts are thrown away.

People like to cook with white flour. This is made by removing the outer husks of the wheat. People like to eat white rice, which has also had its husks removed. The husks of these grains contain most of the nutrients. Brown flour and brown rice are better for us. They are **wholefoods**. Nothing has been taken away from the food or added to it.

In the past, people did not realize that our bodies need the kind of fiber found in brown bread and rice. We have learned about the effect of fiber on the digestive tract. Too little fiber can make us very sick.

▼ Wheat is ground into flour in milling machines. Whole-wheat flour, which includes the husk of the grain, is better for the digestive tract. It adds fiber to the food we eat.

► Animal fat is high in cholesterol. Small amounts are not harmful, but if we always eat too much, it can be unhealthy.

▼ Oils made from sunflower seeds can lower our cholesterol levels. Oils made from peanuts and olives also do not affect the cholesterol level very much.

Unhealthy Food

In countries where there is plenty of food, the food is often processed. Sugar and fat may be added. Our bodies can make use of sugar as a carbohydrate. However, sugar gives the body no other useful nutrients. It does not contain a single mineral or vitamin. It contains no protein or useful fat. Eating sugar does not do our bodies much good. Also, too much sugar makes our teeth decay and extra sugar is stored as fat.

Our bodies need small amounts of certain kinds of fat. When we eat processed food, it is easy to eat more fat than we need. Pies, cookies, cakes, and potato chips all contain lots of hidden fat.

Animal products such as meat, eggs, and milk, contain a fatty substance called **cholesterol**. We need small amounts of cholesterol but too much is bad for us. It clogs up the blood vessels around the heart. It causes heart disease.

In countries where people do not eat large amounts of meat or dairy products, they do not suffer from diseases caused by cholesterol. Vegetable fats contain less cholesterol than animal fats. Eating vegetable-based margarine instead of butter is a good way of cutting down on cholesterol.

35

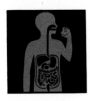

Eating for Health

When a country becomes more developed, the way of life of its citizens often changes. In large cities, everyone seems to be in a hurry. The kind of food people eat changes, too. People buy food that is easy to prepare. It can be taken from a can or a package and eaten quickly.

Foods like this are often called **convenience foods**. Hamburgers, hot dogs, oven-ready French fries, instant snacks, candy bars, and potato chips are all easy to eat. However, if we eat too many of these processed foods, we upset the proper balance of nutrients in our diet.

All Kinds of Food

A healthy diet contains a wide range of different foods. We call it a balanced diet. A balanced diet should include plenty of carbohydrates, especially starch, some protein, and only very small amounts of fat.

The vitamins and fiber needed for a balanced diet should be provided by plenty of fresh fruit and vegetables. There should not be too much sugar or salt added to the diet. We can get all the sugar and salt we need from food just as it is.

◀ The food shown here is just as tasty as processed food, and it is much better for you. A balanced diet often includes wholefoods, which have none of their fiber taken away. The fresher the food, the more likely it is to contain plenty of vitamins.

Planning a Diet

People who study diet and its effect on the body are called **nutritionists**. Ideas about diet have changed in recent years. People used to think that carbohydrates were bad for them and made them fat. Now nutritionists believe that it is all right to get most of your energy from complex carbohydrates like bread, potatoes, or pasta. However, you have to keep down the intake of carbohydrates from fat and sugar.

School Lunches

People's eating habits are made when they are very young. Once you are used to eating very sweet things and lots of fried food, it is not always easy to retrain your tastes.

In many places, nutritionists are making sure that school lunches include more wholefoods and fewer fatty foods. If people are to become healthy adults, and want to stay healthy into old age, they must eat a healthy, balanced diet when they are young.

▲ Candy is all right as an occasional treat, but too much can be bad for you. The sugar causes bacteria to grow in your mouth. The bacteria attack your teeth. Eating candy also makes you have less of an appetite for better foods.

▼ It is especially important for young people, old people, and those who are sick to have a healthy diet. Nutritionists in hospitals have to plan menus carefully.

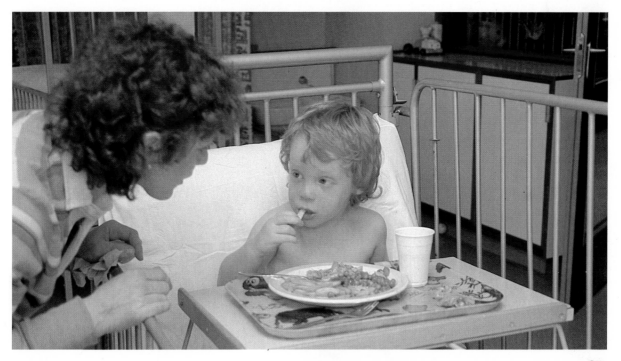

Food and Sickness

▼ Milk may carry the bacteria of several diseases. Most of the milk we drink is pasteurized. It has been heated in large machines like these to destroy the bacteria. Everything is kept very clean.

There are millions of bacteria all around us. They are in the air, on our bodies, and in our food. Many bacteria are helpful. They are used in making cheese, yogurt, wine, and some medicines. Bacteria in our intestines even help us digest our food. However, some bacteria make us sick.

The bacteria have to enter our bodies in order to affect us. If we eat food which contains harmful bacteria, we may become sick.

Some bacteria make poisons as they grow. Others attack the digestive system when we swallow them. Both kinds of bacteria give people **food poisoning**. They may make people vomit. They give people **diarrhea**. Diarrhea makes the body pass out its solid waste matter very often. The body also passes out too much water, which makes the body dry, or dehydrated. These are both ways in which the body gets poison out of its system in a hurry.

Clean Food

Bacteria grow best in moist, warm places. A nice, warm kitchen is ideal! Bacteria are easily spread from our bodies, from animals, and from cuts and grazes. They can easily get onto our hands, and in this way be passed on to our food. **Always wash your hands before touching food.**

When food is cooked well, the bacteria are killed. Fresh food should be covered. Keep cooked food in the refrigerator.

▶ Many people poison their bodies with the things they choose to eat and drink. Alcohol in high amounts can act like a poison, and yet all over the world, people drink too much of it. Too much alcohol damages the liver. This poster, from the Soviet Union, warns people of the dangers of alcohol.

▼ This kind of bacteria are called salmonella. They are sometimes found in red meat and poultry. They can cause vomiting and diarrhea if they are eaten. However, they can be killed by cooking food thoroughly.

ЗЛОУПОТРЕБЛЕНИЕ АЛКОГОЛЕМ

ТАК РАЗВИВАЮТСЯ

ГАСТРИТЫ,
КОЛИТЫ,
ЯЗВЕННАЯ БОЛЕЗНЬ,
ЗАБОЛЕВАНИЯ ПЕЧЕНИ

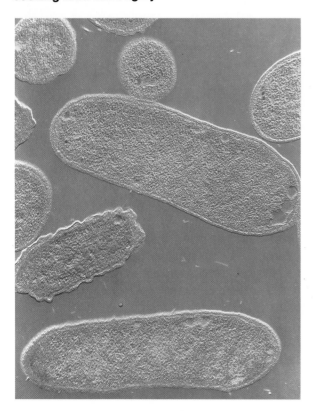

Passing Germs On

Other kinds of bacteria can also pass from one person to another through food. If the cook has a cold and sneezes on the food, anyone eating that food will probably get a cold. Some very serious diseases can be spread by food and through water supplies which contain harmful bacteria. Polio is a disease which can be spread in this way. It can damage people's muscles. Cholera is another disease which is very dangerous. It gives people such bad diarrhea and vomiting that they often die.

In many countries, people are **immunized** against diseases such as these. They are injected with a small amount of the germ. The body makes substances which help it to fight against the disease. These substances stay in the blood, so that the body is protected in the future. If we keep food and water clean, we can help the fight against the spread of disease.

Medicine Today

▼ There are many medicines to soothe upset stomachs. Some upset stomachs can be mild. They just cause slight indigestion. Others are more serious. They have to be treated with antibiotics.

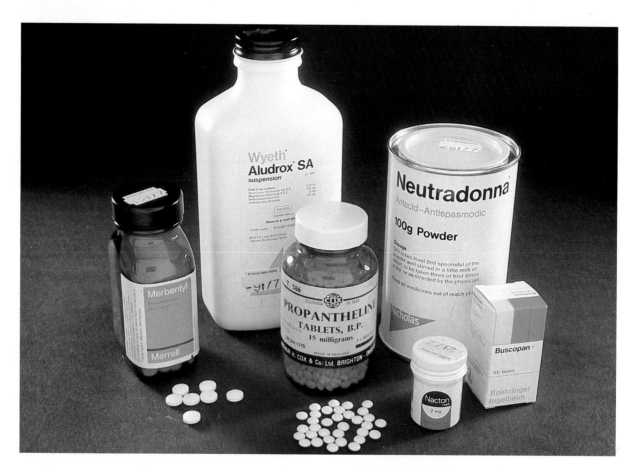

In 1928, a Scottish scientist named Alexander Fleming discovered a powerful new medicine. It was the first of a whole new range of drugs called **antibiotics**. Antibiotics are very useful because they kill bacteria which cause an illness without harming human cells.

Many diseases of the stomach and intestines, such as gastroenteritis, get better by themselves in a day or two. However, bad cases may have to be treated with a course of antibiotics. This kills the bacteria which are causing the disease.

In the Hospital

Surgeons can carry out many different operations on the digestive tract, just as they can on other parts of the body. For example, it is quite common for surgeons to remove an **appendix**. The appendix is a short tube connected to the large intestine.

The appendix is no longer useful to the human body. Sometimes, it becomes infected. This is painful, and it can be dangerous. The appendix has to be taken out before it ruptures, or breaks open.

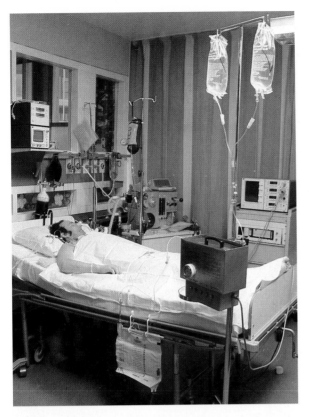

▲ This man is very sick. He is in the hospital. An intravenous drip passes nutrients through tubes straight into his bloodstream.

Providing Nutrients

After some operations, or when people are very sick, they may not be able to digest food properly. The nutrients they need can be fed straight into the patient's bloodstream through an **intravenous drip**. Intravenous means "through a vein." An intravenous drip bypasses the whole digestive system. A liquid containing glucose and salts flows down a tube, and through a needle into one of the patient's veins. The amount of liquid passing into the blood is carefully controlled. Doctors take samples of blood, and test it to make sure that it contains the correct level of glucose and salts.

Machines to the Rescue

If the kidneys stop working properly, dangerous wastes build up in the blood. A **kidney machine** can be used to clean the blood. A living kidney is small enough to fit into one hand. An artificial kidney is a large machine. The patient has to be attached to it for several hours twice a week. Kidney machines have saved countless lives.

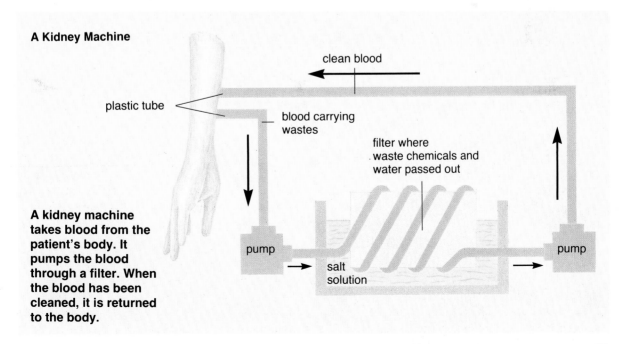

A Kidney Machine

plastic tube

clean blood

blood carrying wastes

filter where waste chemicals and water passed out

pump

salt solution

pump

A kidney machine takes blood from the patient's body. It pumps the blood through a filter. When the blood has been cleaned, it is returned to the body.

Public Health

In many parts of the world, people live in crowded towns and cities. It is easy for bacteria to spread in such places. They can spread in food and in waste. Food preparation and waste disposal must be carefully controlled to prevent the spread of disease.

Getting to Market

Inspectors make sure that food is stored properly before it reaches the stores. Meat, fish, and dairy products must be kept on ice or refrigerated. Grain, fruit, and vegetables must be stored where they cannot be contaminated by insects, rats, or mice.

Buying and Selling

Inspectors make sure that only food of the right quality is put on sale. The next time you go to the supermarket, look carefully at the labels on the food. Most processed food must now be stamped with a date that shows when it must be sold. This makes sure that the customer knows whether the food is fresh or not.

Labels, too, have details of what the food contains. Many processed foods have chemicals added to them. Some of the chemicals are put in to add flavor or color to the food. Others may be added to preserve the food.

▼ Many diseases can be spread by preparing food in dirty places. People who work in kitchens have to keep themselves and everything they use very clean. This hotel food inspector is checking that the rules are being followed.

Scraps of Food

Restaurants and hotels must be inspected also. Their kitchens must be kept clean. Food scraps and other garbage must be removed daily.

Wherever people live, food scraps and garbage must be collected regularly. They must be taken away to a dump where they can be buried or burned. Rotting food attracts flies and spreads disease.

Getting Rid of Waste

Public health also depends on an efficient system of getting rid of human waste. This waste is called **sewage**. It is piped from people's bathrooms to a central sewage plant. There, it is treated with chemicals and filtered to make it harmless. If sewage is not treated before being disposed of, terrible diseases can be spread very easily.

▶ When people are taught to cook, they must also learn how to handle food. Hands must be washed. Stoves, cutlery, dishes, and pans must all be spotless. Bacteria thrive on dirt.

▶ Before sewage plants were built, towns and cities were very unhealthy places. Waste was simply thrown into the streets. Today, sewage is passed through underground pipes to places like this where it can be treated to make it safe.

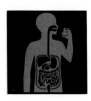

Food in the Future

Today, there are 5 billion people living on the earth. Each year, millions of people die of starvation. By the year 2000, there will be 6.1 billion mouths to feed. How will food be produced for so many people?

Meat or Vegetables?

Wherever we live in the world, we need a balanced diet. The problem is that most of the protein eaten in the more developed countries comes from animals. Rearing animals is a very wasteful way of using the land. Much of the grass that is eaten is used to give the animal energy, rather than just to make protein. It would be better if we could get protein from the plants growing on the land in a more direct way.

Plants like soybeans are a good source of protein. Soybeans have been grown for a long time in Asia. Now, they are being grown in other parts of the world. Soybeans are not very tasty alone, but they can be given flavor. Also, they can be made into a kind of cheese called bean curd, or tofu. Also, they can be made into a substance very much like meat. Soy protein is already added to hamburger. It is an inexpensive way of making it go further. In the future, soybeans could be a good source of protein to supplement the world's food supplies.

▼ In space, there is no air and objects are weightless. However, in the future, it might be possible to build huge spacecraft where crops could be grown and harvested by robots. Scientists have already tried to find out how plants grow on board a spacecraft. This experiment was carried out on the U.S. space shuttle.

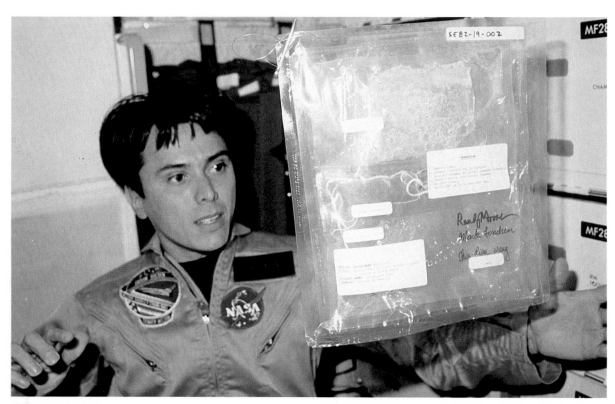

Harvest from the Sea

Most of the food we eat comes from the land, yet the oceans cover two thirds of the world's surface. Catching fish can be a matter of chance. Fish are one of the few creatures that we still have to hunt. However, fish farms are already changing that. Freshwater fish, such as trout, are grown in fish farms, but we need to learn much more about farming fish in the sea. Perhaps, one day, there will be huge farms under the sea, where fish can be bred and seaweed harvested for food.

Food and Science

In the future, there will be new ways of preserving and processing food. Convenience foods will always be popular, but more people will also realize that wholefood is best. New wonder foods may be dreamed up by scientists. All this will be worthwhile only if everyone on the earth has enough food to live a healthy life.

▲ Eilat is in Israel, on the edge of the desert. Irrigation makes it possible to grow crops there. Jets of water are sprayed over the fields.

▼ In the future, farms may be built deep beneath the waves. Fish and shellfish could be grown in large underwater tanks. Seaweed could be grown on the ocean floor and harvested.

45

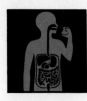

Glossary

amino acids: the important substances the body makes by breaking down the proteins in food.

antibiotics: drugs that can be given to kill bacteria in the body without harming body cells.

appendix: a short tube leading from the large intestine. In animals, it helps digest cellulose, but serves no purpose in humans.

bacteria: tiny creatures that can only be seen with a strong microscope. Many bacteria are helpful to us. Some cause diseases.

bile: a bitter, greenish liquid made in the liver and stored in the gall baldder. Bile helps digest fat.

bladder: the bag in which waste liquid collects before it passes out of the body.

blood vessel: any tube which carries blood through our bodies.

calcium: a substance in the food we eat which builds our bones and teeth.

calorie: a unit for measuring the energy-producing value of food.

canine: one of four sharp, pointed teeth, near the front of the mouth, which are used for tearing food.

capillary: a very tiny tube which carries blood in and out of every part of the body, no matter how small it is.

carbohydrate: a substance made by plants. Animals eat carbohydrate to give them energy.

cell: a very small part or unit of a living animal or plant. Most living things are made up of millions of cells.

chemicals: any substances which can change when joined, or mixed with another substance.

cholesterol: a fatty substance carried in the blood. Too much is unhealthy, and causes heart disease.

colon: another name for the large intestine where water is passed into the body and leaves behind unwanted waste and fiber.

convenience food: food which has been processed, so that it needs little or no preparation before it is eaten.

diarrhea: a disorder of the intestine in which waste matter does not become solid.

diet: the range and kind of foods a person eats.

dietary fiber: the hard, woody parts in the fruit and vegetables we eat. It is not digested, but it gives bulk to our food as it passes through our bodies.

digestion: the process by which food is broken down into simpler forms which can be used in the body as fuel and to build new cells.

digestive tract: the system of tubes which pass food through our body.

duodenum: the part of the intestine that leads out from the stomach. Juices mix with food in the duodenum, and help to digest it.

enzymes: substances made in the body which break food down into simpler parts.

epiglottis: a trapdoor which prevents food from blocking the tubes we breathe through when we swallow.

esophagus: the tube that leads from your throat down to your stomach.

famine: a time when there is little or no food in a country or region because of a disaster like a drought.

fat: one of the basic substances which the body needs to stay healthy. Fat is a source of energy and is found in some plants and all animal foods.

fertilizer: chemicals that are used to make crops grow better.

food chain: the sequence in which one animal eats another animal, and then that animal eats another creature, and so on.

food poisoning: when a person is made sick by the food they have eaten.

food web: a pattern which shows how different animals feed upon each other.

gall bladder: a bag that lies near the small intestine. It acts as a storage area for bile.

gastric juices: liquids which pour into the stomach to help digest food.

glucose: one kind of simple sugar which the body uses as fuel.

glycogen: the form in which glucose is stored in the liver.

hydrochloric acid: a strong liquid found in the stomach. It helps us to digest food.

ileum: the part of the small intestine where digested food is absorbed into the body.

immunize: to give someone a dose of specially-treated germs, so that the body can build up substances to fight the disease.

incisor: one of the sharp, straight teeth at the front of our mouths, for cutting and chopping food.

intravenous drip: a way of passing food and other chemicals directly into someone's bloodstream by using a tube and a needle. Drip-feeding is used when someone is very sick or after a serious operation.

iron: a mineral found in many foods. Our bodies need small amounts of iron to stay healthy.

irradiation: a way of preserving food. Special rays are used to kill any germs in the food.

jaw: the bony parts of the mouth which hold the teeth.

kidney machine: a machine which cleans the blood when a person's kidneys do not work properly.

kidneys: two small organs found on either side of your backbone near your waist. The kidneys filter your blood, and remove wastes and poisons.

large intestine: part of the intestine at the end of the digestive tract where water is taken into the body, leaving behind solid waste.

liver: the body's chemical factory. In the liver, the chemical parts of the food are built up or broken down, so that your body is always supplied with the right nutrients.

malnutrition: a lack of the proper nutrients needed for good health.

minerals: substances, such as iron and calcium, which the body needs in tiny amounts to stay healthy. Small amounts of the minerals are found in many different foods.

molar: one of the teeth at the back of the jaw which are used for grinding food.

molecule: the smallest unit of a substance made up of at least two atoms.

mucus: a jelly-like substance. Mucus coats the walls of the stomach and other organs. It makes the walls slippery and helps protect them.

muscle: a type of material in the body which shortens in order to produce movement.

nitrogen: a substance which the body needs to help build new cells.

nutrients: the basic substances found in all foods which the body uses for fuel, for growth, and for repair.

nutritionist: a person who studies the kinds of food we eat and the nutrients they contain.

organ: a part of the body which has a particular job to do, such as the brain or stomach.

oxygen: a gas found in the air. We need it to breathe. It is used in our bodies, with food, to release the energy we need to stay alive.

pancreas: a small organ found below the stomach. It makes digestive juices which pour into the small intestine.

pesticides: chemicals which are sprayed on crops to kill insects.

portal vein: a large blood vessel which carries blood containing digested food from the small intestine to the liver.

preserve: to treat food to make it last longer.

processed food: food which has been treated, cooked, or preserved.

proteins: one of the basic substances found in food. Proteins are needed to build and repair the body. Meat, eggs, fish, and some parts of plants are rich in protein.

rectum: the end part of the large intestine, where solid waste is passed from the body.

refrigeration: the use of a machine to keep foods at a low temperature.

saliva: the liquid in your mouth. Saliva contains chemicals that start breaking up the food and make it easier to swallow.

salivary gland: one of the small organs under your tongue and inside your cheeks which produce saliva.

sewage: a mixture of water and waste which is carried away from buildings in underground pipes.

small intestine: the first and longest part of the intestine. When food reaches the small intestine, it is finally broken down. The digested food is passed into the body through the wall of the intestine.

soft palate: a flap of skin found at the back of the nose.

sphincter: a circular bunch of muscle which seals the end of various tubes in the body.

starch: a complex carbohydrate found in food such as bread and potatoes.

stomach: the bag-like organ in which food is broken up after being swallowed.

sugar: a carbohydrate found in foods such as fruit, milk, sugarcane, and vegetable roots.

urea: a chemical made in the liver out of protein that we do not need.

ureter: a tube which carries waste from the kidneys to the bladder.

urethra: a tube which carries waste water out of the body from the bladder.

urine: the waste water that passes out of the body.

villus: one of the millions of tiny "fingers" that stick out into the small intestine. Digested food is taken into the bloodstream through the villi.

vitamins: one of a number of complicated chemicals which we need in tiny amounts to stay healthy.

wholefood: food which has had nothing added to it and nothing taken away when we buy it.

Index